DOGS

Anna Pollard

TREASURE
PRESS

YOU ARE WELCOME

EMMANUEL CHRISTIAN FELLOWSHIP

BANK LANE

LERWICK

SUN. 11.00 am - 6.00 pm

CONTENTS

They are a long way from the Arctic but these two young European Wolfspitz belong to the same dog family as the Siberian Husky.

INTRODUCTION

Every dog-lover worth the name thinks of his dog as an honorary human, but how many realize that their pets see them as honorary dogs: as, what is more, pack-leaders who must be respected, followed and obeyed? Man's own view of himself as dog's master would be worthless if the dog did not agree. And, if it had not been for this ancient agreement, man's best friend would never have come on the scene at all.

No one knows exactly when or where man and dog first struck up their working partnership. Some experts point to northern Europe and to a date somewhere between 6000 and 2000 BC; others, to Siberia and to a period that ended over 10,000 years ago. Either way, the dog is easily the first animal that man domesticated.

But what sort of animal was it? Again, there is a mystery. At the moment, there are no less than three main contenders for the title of Original Dog. One set of theories points to the wolf: wolves are easy to tame if caught young enough. But there are snags, the main one being that the canine in question is the common northern wolf of Europe and Asia. How then did the American Indian civilizations come to have domestic dogs?

The second candidate is the golden jackal. Like the common wolf, it is a natural scavenger; in fact, *the* scavenger of the animal world. But, again like the common wolf, it is not native to the western hemisphere.

The third contender is the wild pariah dog that from time out of mind has hung around rubbish-dumps from North Africa to Japan. A near relative occurs in Central and South America. Unlike wolves and jackals, pi dogs, as they are called, have little natural fear of man; while some scientists say this proves that pi dogs are domestic dogs run wild, others feel that the reverse could be true. The despised pariah may yet turn out to be one of man's greatest benefactors.

Whatever the differences between them, there is one thing that wolves, jackals and pi dogs all have in common: they are all social animals. Wolves live and hunt in family groups held together by the tough links of respect and devotion. (Unlike dogs, they pair for life.) Jackals will hunt in packs if they feel like it, and the wild dogs operate exactly like any urban gang. Each dog pack has its own territory and is ready to repel invaders at a moment's notice.

It is this habit of living and working in a group that gave Original Dog – whether wolf, jackal or pariah – its ability to live and work with man. In fact, man was taken over by dog well before dog was formally adopted by man; and, once the bond had been made, the dog was prepared to lavish on its new partner all the loyalty and co-operative spirit that had previously bound it to its natural group and group-leader.

We are not sure of the business details that underpinned that partnership. It is certain that Original Dog and its kind gathered round the encampments of early man and scavenged through the vast, smelly heaps of man's left-overs. It is also certain that Original Dog was present in force when early man went hunting; at the end of the hunt – with luck – came the kill and along with it all the steaming, tasty trimmings that early man couldn't stomach.

What is not certain is early man's part in it all. Up to a point, he would have tolerated the presence of his animal camp-followers. When he went one stage further and encouraged them, did he do it purely because they barked at intruders on their/ his territory? Or did he somehow make use of them on their own hunting trail? Did he follow them as they tracked game, drive them towards it, urge them on as they raced in for the final attack and thus share their victory? Or did he, quite simply, adopt puppies as pets? Pet, hunter, guard: it is probable that Original Dog played not one but all three roles in dealing with its adopted pack. The end result, in any case, was that litter

---

A pleasant expression – as shown opposite – is an official feature of the Golden Retriever breed.

after litter of pups were born that had no inbuilt fear of man at all. Dog – not Original Dog, but the real thing – had arrived.

As co-operation with its human partner developed, Original Dog began to change its shape. Heavy, thickset puppies grew up to make more awesome guards and killers than those that were slim and light: a guard dog's owner, noticing this, would do all he could to encourage the heavy, thickset type. In the same way, stream-lined speedy dogs would be prized for the way they could run a quarry down. Very gradually, the world's first breeds of dog came into being.

These were of two kinds to begin with: a large, ferocious type built on the lines of a Mastiff, and a long-legged, tucked-up animal very like a modern Greyhound. The Assyrians and Babylonians had both and so did the ancient Egyptians. The Assyrian Mastiff in particular led a fearsomely dangerous life; it was used for hunting lions.

The first evidence we have of the two Egyptian breeds dates from before 3000 BC. In the next two thousand years, more breeds emerged: a curly-tailed dog like a Chow, a hound with floppy ears, a Wolf-hound, a short-legged Terrier, and the ancestor of the oldest breed still in existence, the Saluki. The Egyptian Greyhound type was, of course, still going strong; one Pharaoh had a special favorite called White Gazelle. Even after 4000 years, it is a fine name for a Greyhound.

The ancient Greeks also took dog-owning seriously. They had all the established breeds of the time, and evolved a new one rather like a modern Pointer. Alexander the Great became so fond of one that he had bred that he took it everywhere, and when it tangled with an elephant during a battle and was killed, its royal owner gave the dog a state funeral.

The odd thing is that today's dog-owners will find it easier to understand Alexander's feelings than his contemporaries did. With rare exceptions, the dogs of ancient Greeks – along with everybody else's dogs, right up to the last century – were not really regarded with much love. Useful, ornamental, even fashionable, yes; but man's best friend – no. For, like their earliest ancestors in man's service, most dogs were reared in order to work, and work they did; as herders, war dogs (the Babylonians were the first to think of this), as dogs to pull things, guard things, chase things. For hundreds of years, members of the Husky family had been transporting man and his goods across the frozen wastes of the far north, and eventually draught dogs came to central and western Europe, and were used for pulling light carts.

The occupation of guard dog is equally ancient: the Romans – like the rest of the world at that time – thought highly of the giant Mastiff breed they called *pugnaces molossi*, or 'the battlers', and later ages echoed this approval. (Unhappily, the dogs of Imperial Rome fought too well for their own good: particularly ferocious specimens were matched against each other in the Colosseum to make a Roman holiday.)

As for hunting, it gradually diminished as man's chief way of filling his larder. But at the same time, it continued as an extremely prestigious sport. As time went on, kennels throughout the world were slowly filled with more and more breeds of dog, all designed for one particular sporting activity or another. First came the Greyhounds, which hunted by sight and specialized in chasing hares; then the ancestors of our modern hounds that hunt by scent. (The Bloodhound, grandfather of all scent hounds as far as Europe and the West is concerned, descends from dogs first bred by the holy St Hubert of France.)

Falconry first brought game dogs into existence, but the development of the gun touched off a breeding boom that produced Spaniels, Setters, Retrievers and Poodles.

Alongside these aristocrats of the sporting world ran a large and jolly army of canines that were used for the dual purpose of sport and killing vermin. They were the terriers: tough, friendly, game for anything.

But – again unhappily – these too got mixed up in the animal fights that delighted mobs until the 19th century. In the same way that Bulldogs were developed for baiting bulls, Bull Terriers and their Staffordshire cousins were developed for baiting each other.

Dog-fighting contests have now been made illegal, of course, and the fact that it fills us with disgust is proof of the immense change that has overtaken our views on animals in the last 100 years or so. All animals have benefited from this transformation of attitude, but dogs have benefited in a very special way.

All along, dogs have offered their masters amazing quantities of loyalty, friendship and willingness to help; at last, the friendship is being returned. On top of that, we are finally beginning to appreciate just how much dogs have been contributing to the alliance, and for how long. We have begun to pay off the debt – but, generous as ever, Dog is not pressing for payment and dog-owners will agree that its patience does them honor.

The elegant Saluki (*below*) is the oldest recorded breed still in existence. Its history dates back over 5000 years. The ancient Egyptians had Salukis, and so did the people of Mesopotamia. In both cases, they used their dogs for hunting deer. The modern Saluki is less heavily built than its distant ancestors, and its other name – Gazelle Hound – gives an idea of what it can do on the hunting field. It is a dog that works by sight rather than by scent, it can out-run all but the speediest and most elusive quarry that it can find.

KNOW YOUR DOG

The Chow below has a chunky body, fluffy coat and pricked ears. When it stands up, its tail will make a tight curl over its back. In contrast, the Irish Setters opposite have slender bodies, flat coats, drop ears and straight tails. On the face of it, Chows and Setters have only one thing in common: both are dogs. There are over 200 breeds of dog now in existence, and the dogs themselves display a staggering variety of sizes and shapes. There are small dogs and big ones, solid dogs and slim ones, sociable dogs and aloof ones. The following pages explore some of the many variations on the canine theme.

The basic types

The three breeds shown here represent the three basic types from which all the others sprang.

The European Spitz (*top left*) is related to the Chow, the Samoyed, the Malamutes and Eskimo Dogs of the far north, to the 'barkless' Basenji of Africa (which yodels rather than barks), and to the Pomeranian.

The Greyhound (*below left*) comes from the same family as – among others – the Afghan, the Borzoi, the Saluki and the enormous Irish Wolfhound (one of the biggest dogs in the world).

The Alsatian (*below*) – whose proper name is the German Shepherd Dog – is a member of the large group of dogs that was first brought into being for guarding and herding livestock.

Others in the same family are the Collie, the Old English Sheepdog, the Shetland Sheepdog, the Groenendael and the Malinois (both Belgian shepherd dogs), the Australian Kelpie and Blue Heeler, the Pyrenean Mountain Dog, the Corgi and the Maltese. Although they vary in size and appearance, all of them are classed as 'pastoral dogs'.

Although the Basenji has a short coat, most members of the Spitz family have the deep, thick fur of the dog shown left. The pricked ears, pointed muzzle and tightly curled tail are other typical features. So are the strong neck and medium-length legs. Many Spitz dogs have round, cat-like feet but the sledge-pullers like the Samoyed and the Husky are exceptions. Long feet in a Greyhound, however, are a definite fault. The whole tribe are built and bred for speed, and 'cat feet' are better adapted to fast running over long distances and hard ground.

The riddle posed by the Australian Dingo (*overleaf*) has puzzled scientists for years. It was the only non-marsupial mammal found there.

Profiles

Two sporting breeds, two working breeds, and one that is strictly ornamental: the six dogs shown on the right between them sum up the practical reasons why the relationship between man and dog has flourished.

Sharply-pricked ears are an important feature of the Schnauzer (*top right*). The breed originated over 300 years ago in Germany, and there is also a miniature version. Experts are divided as to whether Schnauzers are terriers or pastoral dogs. Although they have a strong terrier look about them, they have proved their worth as herders of cattle – a fact that puts them squarely among the workers.

The Airedale (*below right*) is a true terrier, and for this reason is classified as a sporting dog. An exception to the general terrier tendency towards shortness of leg, Airedales stand about 23in (58cm) high at the shoulder and can weigh up to 50lb (22·5kg).

Another sporting dog, the Beagle (*opposite, top left*) is one of the scent hounds. Its speciality is hunting hares. Smaller in size than the Foxhound, it also belongs to a much older breed. In England – where the breed originated – it was being used for hunting as early as the Saxon period. It is now very popular as a pet.

Odd-dog-out among these portraits of working and sporting dogs, is the Pug (*opposite, top right*), a miniature or 'toy' breed, developed purely for its engaging looks. British households were keeping pet Pugs in the time of Elizabeth I. Like the Bulldog and the Boxer, it is a member of the very ancient Mastiff family.

A white dog is difficult to see among a flock of white sheep and, for this reason, sheepdogs the world over tend to be dark in color. The Hungarian (*opposite, below*) demonstrates the rule.

As lovers of the breed know, the fierce-looking Boxer (*below*) is in fact one of the most pleasant-tempered dogs in the world. Intelligent, loyal and affectionate, Boxers are extremely popular pets, and also make good guard dogs. The short muzzle is a hallmark of the breed, as is the broad head and the pronounced 'stop' between the eyes. All Boxers have their tails docked short in puppyhood and in some countries the ears are cropped as well. Ear-cropping, which makes the ears stand up straight, is not allowed in countries such as Great Britain.

The Golden Labrador Retriever (*opposite, top left*) is another dog with a huge following of enthusiasts. Like all gundogs, it has an equable, steady temperament; its intelligence also fits it for guide-dog work with blind people. A Labrador that has been well trained as a retriever can pick up a snowball without

breaking it – or even an egg.

Most terriers are small, close-to-the-ground dogs, but the Bedlington (*opposite, top right*) is an exception. Standing still, it is often mistaken for a large lamb; when it runs, its long legs give it a greyhound-like gait. The fluffy top-knot on the forehead is an important Bedlington characteristic, as are the fringed ears.

A sledge-dog with a difference: the Samoyed (*below opposite*) is also used in the far north of Russia for herding reindeer, hunting and guarding. The breed is at least 1000 years old, and probably much older. Like all Spitz-type dogs, Samoyeds have erect ears and a curled tail. But their smiling expression is a Samoyed speciality. Their Russian name has a curious meaning: 'Self-eater', hinting at the savage early history of the breed.

Big dogs...

Some dogs are so small that they can be carried in one hand. Others are so enormous that they cannot be carried at all – unless their owners also have a truck. The Afghan Hound (*below*), although not as big as some dogs, would certainly make all but the strongest men think twice about picking it up: it measures up to 29in (68·5cm) at the shoulder and weighs about 65lb (30kg).

The Irish Wolfhound (*opposite*) is larger still. Its minimum shoulder height is 31in (78cm), and its minimum weight is 120lb (55kg). It is one of the largest breeds in the world.

Both Afghans and Wolfhounds are members of the Greyhound family. Under that long coat, the Afghan has a 'tucked up' outline in the typical Greyhound style. Like the Greyhound again, both hunt by sight. The Wolfhound is now rare.

Although most of the world's tallest dogs belong to the Greyhound group, the world's heaviest dogs tend to come from a completely different family: that of the Mastiffs. The St Bernard (*right*) has a lower shoulder height than the Irish Wolfhound, but weighs a great deal more. Adult dogs average out at about 200lb (90kg). Its cousin, the Pyrenean Mountain Dog (*below*), stands up to 32in (81cm) high and weighs 120lb (55kg) or more.

The original function of Mastiff-type dogs was to stand guard over flocks and property, and scare away intruders. A great turn of speed was not essential, but size, strength and holding-power were: a dog standing guard over a flock of sheep might have to deal with a wolf one day, a bear the next. In spite of their strength, though, most members of the Mastiff family are extremely good natured and docile. The gigantic St Bernard is possibly the best natured of the whole group – but the popular story about its life-saving activities is a fiction. Its real use was as a mountain guide dog. The alpine rescue services of today tend to use sheepdogs of the Alsatian or Groenendael breeds.

...and little dogs

The Wire-haired Dachshund (*opposite*) is not a terrier, but one of the smallest of the hound family. His miniature cousin, which should weigh no more than 12lb (5·5kg), is only half its size – but both appear large when compared to the tiny Chihuahua (*below, left*).

With a maximum weight of 6lb (2·5kg), Chihuahuas are one of the world's smallest dogs, and the Yorkshire Terrier (*top, left*) and the Pekingese (*left, middle picture*) are not much bigger.

All three are toy breeds; others include the Pug (a toy Mastiff), the Pomeranian (a toy Spitz), the Italian Greyhound (a Greyhound in miniature) and the King Charles Spaniel.

Like most terriers, the Yorkshire was originally bred to catch vermin: in this case, rats. A modern prize-winning dog will weigh no more than 7lb (3kg), and will have exceptionally long, silky hair. But it will still display the tough, take-on-anything character of its sporting ancestors.

The Pekingese has a more exotic past. The breed dates back to the seventh century AD, and – as the name implies – originated in China. On account of its courage and its luxurious coat, the Chinese used to call it the 'lion dog'. Really tiny specimens were particularly valuable: during the winter, owners carried them in their sleeves and used them as living hand-warmers.

The Chihuahua is one of the few breeds that originated in the New World (another is the much larger Boston Terrier). When the Spanish *conquistadores* invaded Mexico, they found that the Indians both ate dogs and kept them as pets. The modern Chihuahua (pronounced chee-wah-wah) usually has a short, glossy coat, but longer coats are allowed.

DOG FAMILIES

There are few things as pleasing as a puppy – unless it is two puppies, or three, or four, or five . . . In general, small dogs have small families, large dogs have large ones. Really large dogs such as Great Danes sometimes give birth to eight or more pups. The single pup of the Boxer couple opposite is an exception to the rule. The four young Poodles below make up an average-sized family for a small or medium-sized dog. They will stay with their mother until they are two months old; then they will be off to their new owners. In a year or so, they will be capable of having families of their own.

Twins

The Wire-haired Fox Terrier pups below look
alike, are alike. In fact, they are identical twins,
born within 30 minutes of each other. They
have come a long way, though, since those early
days when they did nothing but feed and sleep;
they are now all set to make their presence felt
in the outside world.

Triplets

Some puppies look like their parents; others look like nothing on earth. The trio below are not young bears, young wombats or young Persian cats; they are young Chows. As with all dogs, snub noses and floppy ears are marks of babyhood; in some breeds, these features are kept throughout life.

Quads

Companions

Dogs have two sorts of families: their own, and their owners'. Indeed, from the dog's point of view, its owner is the undisputed pack-leader or family chieftain, and the owner's relatives are generally accepted in the same spirit.

The family circle can also include other dogs. The Cocker Spaniel, the Dalmatian and the Collie below could well be inseparable, and form a miniature pack that functions exactly like a human gang. Cats are a different matter – but the Entlebuch Hound opposite proves that a cat-and-dog life can be quite a peaceful affair. Like most dogs who live under the same roof as a cat, it has adopted the household tabby as a sort of non-canine pack-member. Cats tend to take a more ambivalent view of such a relationship, but they are usually prepared to at least tolerate much bigger companions even if they do not become fond of them.

CARING FOR YOUR DOG

GETTING A DOG

Before you get a dog be sure to pick a type that is right for you. Some – especially the sporting breeds – need a great deal of exercise. Bouncy terriers can be a worry to the elderly; the scent hounds have a tendency to stray; longhaired breeds need special attention paid to their grooming. A big dog will swamp a small house and will incur a large food bill.

When buying a puppy, it is best to go to a breeder rather than a pet shop. Breeders often advertise in local papers. Try to see the whole litter of pups before choosing one, and take a look at the mother as well.

No puppy should be taken away from its mother before it is two months old.

FEEDING

Many owners feed a commercially prepared 'all-in-one' dried food which contains all a dog needs for a balanced diet. 'All-in-one' food is also sold moist or in cans.

The traditional way of feeding dogs is on meat (butcher's or canned), supplemented by dog biscuits. Offal should be cooked first but fresh meat (other than rabbit and pork) can be fed raw.

Medium-sized and small dogs prefer to be fed morning and evening. Large dogs – which are equipped to take in their day's food at one go – are often fed in the evening only. The quantity of solids fed daily depends on the size of the dog; it can range from a few grams or ounces in the case of a toy breed to 3^{lb} ($1 \cdot 5kg$) or more for a Great Dane. (See also page 56.)

Dogs appreciate a bone to chew; this is particularly important if their normal diet is rather soft. The only safe bones are large ones: shin, shank or knuckle. Dog-chews (available from pet shops) are an alternative.

Fresh water should be available at all times. Never give chop, poultry or game bones; they can splinter and stick in the dog's throat.

GENERAL MANAGEMENT

Apart from food and water, a dog has three basic requirements. These are: a comfortable sleeping-place, a safe area for free exercise, and as much accompanied exercise as it can take.

All pet shops sell dog-beds and baskets; choose one that is big enough for your dog, line it with newspaper covered by a rug and place it in a draught-free spot.

All dogs need to go out first thing in the morning to urinate; they also need space to roam around in during the day. A dog's daily stint of exercise must never be skipped.

TRAINING

This is an immense subject on which every owner has his or her theories but the basic keys to successful training are patience and praise; the dog has a fundamental urge to please you, so he is on your side before you even start.

Praise a dog *every* time he gets something right; it is this that will really fix good habits in his mind.

When things go wrong, scold rather than slap. A slap will make a puppy nervous and could also injure him. Use as deep a voice as possible for scolding.

For praise, use your normal voice and try to stick to the same words each time.

Training starts at about eight weeks, when a puppy is old enough to master the basics of house-training. One simple method of doing this is to put him outside first thing in the morning, after every meal and after a sleep or any bout of activity. Watch him carefully; you will soon recognize the signals he makes when he wants to urinate.

Praise him when he passes water or motions outdoors; scold him if he makes a mistake in the house. An exception to the rule is if a puppy dribbles when over-excited or when introduced to strangers. This is an involuntary reaction and should not be seen as an offense.

Pups should also, at the very least, learn to obey the commands 'Sit', 'Heel', and 'Come'. Train a pup to sit by saying the command and pushing his hindquarters down at the same time.

'Heel' is done on the lead: the pup is gently pulled into the 'heel' position each time he strays off.

Start the first stage of 'Come' when the pup is clearly about to race up to you. Say 'Come', and praise him when he does. Later, fix a long string to his collar, say 'Come', and gently gather him in.

Repeat the training sessions several times a day but always keep them very short. Remember that success must *always* be rewarded with praise.

ILLNESSES

Before you get a dog it is wise to find out where the local veterinarian lives. The reason is that all puppies should be innoculated against the very serious diseases – distemper, hardpad, infectious hepatitis, leptospirosis and tetanus. The breeder from whom you get your pup may have had this done already; find out.

Booster injections will be needed annually and your vet will tell you if he thinks any other types of immunization are advisable. In particular, ask him about protection against rabies, which can also be transmitted to humans.

Other dog illnesses include pneumonia, colds, bronchitis and skin ailments such as eczema and ringworm. Ringworm, too, can be passed on to humans.

A dog may pick up fleas or lice. These can be treated with a flea powder specifically intended for pets. Read the label to check that dogs are included, and follow the maker's instructions carefully. Suspect ear mites (canker) if the dog shakes his head or rubs his ears continually, and have him treated professionally.

A flea-ridden dog risks getting tapeworms. Segments of tapeworm – like grains of rice – are likely to be visible under the dog's tail or in his bed. In addition, the dog may vomit, drag his hindquarters along the floor and look out of condition.

Puppies are particularly susceptible to another internal parasite, the roundworm. When passed in the pup's motions, it looks like a thin piece (or pieces) of string. A pot belly is another sign of worms. Again, take your dog to the vet if you think he has either of these.

After handling a dog that is out-of-sorts in any way, be particularly careful to wash your hands thoroughly. Anyone nursing a sick dog should wear an overall and, in the case of ringworm, gloves.

FEMALES ON HEAT

The average female dog comes on heat twice yearly. Since she is now ready to mate, she will be followed by dogs each time she is taken for a walk.

One way of preventing unwanted pregnancies is to keep her confined to an intruder-proof yard. Another is to have her boarded out for the whole period. A third alternative is to have her spayed. A spayed animal cannot come on heat or have puppies; she will also, however, be barred from the show ring.

DOG LAWS

The basic attitude of the law to dogs is that they MUST be kept under control at all times. Other legal obligations of dog-owners may include the responsibility of buying a licence for their pet, and making sure he wears a collar.

Collars should fit snugly but not tightly and you should be able to put two fingers between the collar and the dog's neck.

In most urban areas there are regulations against dogs fouling the sidewalks. There may also be a regulation against dogs roaming unescorted; it is, in any case, dangerous to allow your dog to do this.

WORKING DOGS

On Germany's Lüneburg Heath, a shepherd and his dogs prepare for a day's work. It is a scene that has been repeated millions of times. The dog's main partner in the exercise is the man who trained it. Their association marks one of the peaks in man's relationships with animals.

Sporting dogs

The Golden Retriever (*below*) and the Irish Setter (*opposite*) are breeds that were first developed to perform a useful service for man and, like many other members of their families, the two dogs shown here are highly trained. The job they do is very specialized, and there are many breeds doing work along the same lines. The whole group has been classified for centuries as sporting dogs rather than working dogs. The Bloodhound, the Beagle, the Foxhound, the Deerhound and the Greyhound are all sporting dogs, as are more exotic relations like the Afghan. The terriers count as sporting dogs too.

The Setter's job involves seeking out game, waiting until its master arrives, and then startling the bird so that it flies up. The Retriever brings the dead bird back to the sportsman without damaging it.

The three-cornered relationship (*top*) of falconer, bird, and dogs is a living reminder of how gundog training first started. Before firearms became a practical possibility for the sportsman, the falcon performed the same role as a bullet. But a dog was always needed to find the game and to flush it.

The Setter's job had, therefore, come into being before both guns and Setters arrived on the scene. Setters were originally called Setting Spaniels. The first dogs to be specifically bred for working with guns, they are trained to go through the same find-and-flush routine as the falconer's dog, but with one important difference. Having found a bird, the dog has to wait for the arrival of its master before flushing it. While waiting, Setters drop to the ground in a crouch. Pointers – which were developed shortly afterwards – 'point' standing up, with their nose indicating the location of game. Only when the sportsman arrives does either breed move forward to make the game fly up.

Both Setters and Pointers are trained to stay close to their masters except when directed to do their jobs. The German Shorthaired Pointer on the left is behaving perfectly. The same goes for retrieving dogs like the one opposite. A dog that is here, there, and everywhere while guns are going off cannot expect to live long. The Retriever group includes the Spaniels (who also do the job of a Setter), the Retrievers themselves, and the Poodle, which was first bred to retrieve ducks from the water.

Two Tennessee farmers and their dogs prepare for a hunt. It could be for raccoons, oppossum or a variety of vermin. The dogs themselves are not quite Greyhounds, not quite anything, but they are all expert hunters and – as their Greyhound-like physique indicates – they are built for speed. Their nearest relative might be the British Lurcher, an 'unofficial' breed that has a centuries-long history. The Lurcher is the traditional dog of the gypsies: it looks like a wire-haired Greyhound, and has all the Greyhound's abilities for hunting game by sight. On both the hunting-field and the race-track, the Greyhound's proper prey is hare (the race-track hare is, of course, an electric one). But, as their names often indicate, the other members of the sight hound family have in the past been used for much bigger game. The Saluki was sent after gazelles, the Irish Wolfhound and the Russian Borzoi after wolves. The Deerhound – which looks like the Irish Wolfhound but is slightly smaller – was a deer-hunter. And the heavily built Rhodesian Ridgeback of Africa was used for hunting lions.

For over 1000 years, the hound group of sporting dogs has been divided into two sections: dogs that hunt by sight, and dogs that hunt by scent. Greyhounds and Lurchers are typical sight hounds, and usually work on their own or in pairs; Foxhounds, Beagles and Bassets are all scent hounds, and always work in a pack. Although the hounds and huntsmen opposite are a traditional part of the English country scene, organized fox-hunting is in fact a relatively new field sport. It only started to become generally popular in the 18th century. The dogs are carefully trained to work as a pack; they are never kept as pets, although puppies are boarded out in private homes until they begin their pack training. The families who take them on are known as 'puppy walkers'. One of the taller members of the hound family, the Foxhound, can keep going for 60 miles (96km) or more in a day without collapsing.

Otter hunting (*below*) is very much older than fox-hunting. Otter hounds have the distinctly un-canine feature of webbed feet.

44

Snow dogs

For a European, the St Bernard (*below, left*) is a fine example of the snow dog. Equipped with its barrel of brandy, it is supposed to act as a mountain rescue dog, digging out travellers who have been buried in snowdrifts. Although its thick coat certainly fits it for working in the cold, it would actually be as unhappy in a snowdrift as a human, if not more so. A St Bernard weighs as much as a heavy man, and, even though this weight is carried on four feet rather than two, it would still trap the dog in any drift it encountered. On hard snow, the St Bernard is much happier, and more useful, since its huge paws help it to grip the ground firmly.

The Eskimo Dogs of the far north are true snow dogs, bred and trained for pulling sledges. The Greenland sledge-team shown opposite (*top left*) is linked in the traditional 'fan hitch'; each dog is harnessed separately to the sledge, and the team spreads out like a fan when it is travelling. Another harnessing system is the 'Western hitch', in which each dog is linked to a long line, with the lead dog at its head.

In all, there are four Husky breeds: the Eskimo Dog, the Malamute, the Samoyed and the Siberian Husky (*below*). Although their job has to some extent been taken over by mechanized transport, there are still areas in the world where the Eskimo and the others play an essential role. In addition, the Samoyed is firmly established everywhere as a popular pet, while both the Malamute and the Siberian have large followings among dog-owners in the USA.

Guard dogs

Highly intelligent dogs, like Alsatians, are often used for army, police and guard-dog work. Not only do Alsatians combine suspicion of strangers with extreme loyalty to their master or handler; they also have powers that the most alert of humans cannot acquire. For example, their sense of hearing is so acute it can capture noises seven octaves beyond the range of the human ear. They are also nimbler than humans, and can work better in darkness.

All working dogs of this type are very carefully trained: training exercises in height and hurdle work are shown on the left. An important part of training is 'manwork', in which the dog is taught to hold (*not* savage) a suspect.

DOG'S LIFE

Dogs have come a long way since they ran with the pack through dim forests or stony wasteland. The Terrier below and the Spaniel opposite are both leading a modern dog's life, and are thoroughly happy about it. (The Spaniel's friend is also quite at ease in her pet's world.)
The town Terrier, like customers at the café across the road, finds the urban scene full of interest, while his opposite number in the country is just as contented. A dog's main needs are food, exercise and affection; as long as it gets all three, it will be prepared to go anywhere. A dog that is looked after properly will be a devoted and affectionate member of the family.

A sight hound in the desert: this 20th-century dog carries 5000 years of canine memories in its blood. The ancient Egyptians had dogs like this, and so did the huntsmen of the Assyrian and Babylonian empires. Its long legs are a promise of huge sprinting powers; its jaws are strong enough to hold its prey. Its slender body and short coat are well suited to withstand the desert heat. And that keen stare will miss nothing that flashes across the horizon.

At the moment, however, this dog with a history is not interested in hunting: as its pose indicates, what it wants is a game.

For hundreds of years, the dog's life led by the two shaggy breeds on the right was a hard-working and even dangerous one. The shaggier of the pair – the Hungarian Komondor (on the left) was developed to guard flocks both from thieves and from predators like bears and wolves. The Old English Sheepdog had it easier, but only slightly: it accompanied English livestock drovers on their long treks to sales and fairs. The Old English Sheepdog is also called the Bobtail.

Although both breeds are old, the Komondor is by far the older of the two. Its history as a pastoral guard dog goes back at least 1000 years. Like many other flock-guarding breeds, it is both solidly built and very large. A fully grown dog can measure 32in (81cm) to the shoulder – a figure that puts it in the same size bracket as the Great Dane.

The long, thick hair of both sheepdogs is an essential protection against bad weather. Dense coats are also a feature of the Rough and Border Collies and the Shetland Sheepdog.

Food

A dog's interest in food starts literally at birth. After being cleaned by its mother, a pup noses round until it finds her belly. (The search is done entirely by touch; puppies are born blind and deaf.) When it locates a teat, it will instinctively attach itself and then begin to suck. The mother provides all the pups' food (*opposite*, *top left*) until they are four weeks old. At this point, though, they start needing solids: minced-up meat, moistened puppy meal and milky foods. It is at this point, too, that they start learning to eat from a dish (*below*) or dog-bowl (*opposite*, *top right*). Snub-nosed dogs like Pugs are much happier with a shallow bowl, but Hounds, Spaniels (*below right*) and the like can cope quite easily with a deeper container. Weaning is over when the pups are seven weeks old. From then until the age of four months, they need four small meals a day. Between four and eight months, they will eat three times a day; between eight and ten months, they should be fed twice daily, with a bowl of milk between their meals.

The full adult feeding program starts when a dog is between 10 months and a year old. Some dogs are fed twice a day; others – especially the larger breeds – get their whole daily ration in one helping. The amount fed depends on the size of the dog.

A dog's main food is meat, supplemented by dog biscuits. Grocers and petshops also stock commercially prepared foods, some of which form complete diets in themselves. Fresh water should always be available (see also Caring for Your Dog).

Play

Most dogs enjoy a game, and, as with children, anything does for a plaything: sticks, stones, water, a ball, rags, shoes, gloves, bedding, or each other. Up to a point, a dog at play is practising skills like hunting and killing, and its playthings are substitutes for live prey. A puppy's mock fights, too, are practice bouts for real situations in the dog's adult life.

But some dogs seem to carry their games several stages further. A few develop a superior form of retrieving: using a sideways flick of the muzzle, it is the dog that throws the ball – and it is the owner who retrieves it.

Others, again, turn the 'seeking game' on its head by getting an owner to do the seeking (the dog, meanwhile, stealthily follows on the owner's heels), but this is not so much playing a game as playing a joke – a higher form of activity altogether.

59

Activities

The Rough Collie (*opposite*) appears to be taking its ease in the sun. But appearances are deceptive. It is, in fact, engaging in what is possibly the most important dog activity of all: observing its environment. In addition to watching the world go by, it is hearing it, feeling it, smelling it, and adding up the messages it receives to get an overall picture of its surroundings. What kind of picture is being assembled in the dog's brain?

It is not a picture that would make much sense to us – at first. There is, for example, very little colour in it (dogs are believed to be colour-blind). Noises are louder, higher, more complicated. And the messages taken in through the nose are more complicated still. No human can really begin to comprehend what a dog's sense of smell means to it. Nor can we really imagine what the dog makes of it all. However

60

close the relationship between a dog and its owner – and however much the owner knows about dogs in general – there are always vast areas of experience on the dog's part that remain closed territory to non-dogs. One of the places where dogs and humans can meet on equal terms is in water. Neither can live in it, but both enjoy venturing into it for short spells. The Wire-haired Dachshund demonstrates the efficient swimming technique adopted by all canines: the dog-paddle, one of the first strokes attempted by humans as well.

Many of a domestic dog's activities depend on man. Man – or woman – grooms it (*top left*), feeds it (*bottom left*), exercises it. But, to be really contented, a dog needs the chance to strike out sometimes on an individual line of his own. The dog on the opposite page will soon emerge empty-mouthed, muddy and thoroughly happy. The terrier which digs up flower-beds is expressing itself in the same way, and so is the Beagle which vanishes over the horizon after a scent of which its owner is unaware.

Time, safety, neighbors' feelings, and the law all impose obvious (and strict) limitations on the amount of self-expression a dog can be allowed. But all good owners will allow it as much as they can – and be prepared to wash the mud off afterwards.

INDEX

FRONT COVER PHOTOGRAPH: OCTOPUS GROUP/PETER LOUGHRAN
BACK COVER PHOTOGRAPH: R. WILLBIE/ANIMAL PHOTOGRAPHY

This edition published in 1990 by Treasure Press, Michelin House, 81 Fulham Road, London SW3 6RB

© 1979 Cathay Books

ISBN 1 85051 487 9

Produced by Mandarin Offset
Printed in Hong Kong